REMAINS

JESÚS CASTILLO

McSWEENEY'S
POETRY SERIES

McSWEENEY'S

SAN FRANCISCO

www.mcsweeneys.net

Copyright © 2016 Jesús Castillo

Cover art and frontispiece by Hannah E. Morris.

The McSweeney's Poetry Series is edited by Dominic Luxford and Jesse Nathan.

The editors wish to thank assistant editor Rachel Z. Arndt, editorial interns Jess Bergman, Alison Castleman, Andrew Colarusso, Lizzie Davis, Waylon Elder, Megan Freshley, Gabriel Ojeda-Sague, Neesa Sonoquie, and copyeditor Britta Ameel.

McSweeney's and colophon are registered trademarks of McSweeney's, an independent publisher with wildly fluctuating resources.

ISBN 978-1-940450-42-1

Printed in the United States.

This is a test. A set of margins created
for company. For waiting in train stations
or asking a stranger the time. You're allowed
to freak out this much only. There's a green car
parked outside, by the curb, near the bike racks.
An old man is asking people to put
change in his plastic cup, and I remember
my name contains both my father's and
grandfather's stories. The table I'm sitting at
is made of steel and marble. It's cold and it's
spring. In the song on the radio, a noise

•

Carmen. Do you remember Carmen? My cousin
who married young to a man twice her age and with
little means. Back in San Luis. I don't know
exactly how it happened, but the farm I remember,
the pond overgrown with stalks and moss.
Where I'd catch dragonflies by their tails. Their wings
almost metallic in the gilded, orange noon. Carmen,
still 15 and a virgin, sang in the straw-roofed kitchen hut,
where she helped our grandmother cook, steaming
the pig's tripe or grinding corn into mush.

•

At some point, air support was requested. It was
mostly children. But the claims were exaggerated.
140 casualties, in this instance, is an acceptable
mode of living. The captain hacked and spit like an old
engine on a cold morning. When it rains, the homeless
will sit in the shelter of bus stops for hours, sometimes
even long after it's cleared. I know I call in a time
of brittle language. I know the dams gather floods,
and there's comfort in the precision of machines.
Is painterly kindness enough? Or what is it, exactly,
that we're saving from extinction?

Is this Chopin? As we drive in the valleys,
graves. Insistent string. Mountain ridges opening up
to reveal cloud formations rifting. Music
as a gesture outwards or a vague suspicion
of what we were. I say this now as my body, which appears
young, goes on collecting small disjunctions.
I say this as a breath rising up to the wooden beams
of a restaurant ceiling. A rhythm like glass beads
raining on tile. Days like passages in a Russian novel
where love is a distant fracture we can hear from our beds.

.

On the drive through the redwoods, I don't know
if you recall. A harmonica note held for a summer,
truer than the blanket uncertainty we learn to live with.
The fog making the road the edge of the world.
Our senses broke and scenes began to sputter.
We looked under the seats for a map or a booklet
that might help. The grandchildren will learn
about failure soon. It's that age. So will they sense
in that moment a well of song? Will they know
what we meant by sorrows or jest?

.

The collision, the rain slowing, the pebble breaking,
the slope of a hip, the skylight's glare, the tedium
of age, the building full of children, the repetitive
mechanism, the idle company, the phone call,
the steps, the evening walk's end, the minute space
between two things touching, the loss of meaning,
the boundary's approach, the rendering of limbs,
the edge of remembered towns,

It rained for days. Our hands were covered
in the smell of April. I forgot the time
and place of departure. I was finally free to go.
I was hungry and bad at honesty, attempting still to break
through the blank space. Eternity's other shore.
A place to wake from one's portrait. A place
with enough memory to store our lives' echoes
thus far.

·

My friends and I wanted some way
to see our wreckage as material for a world.
So we put on our coats and headed to the cemetery
on a bright afternoon. Tulip gardens patched
the hills. Young couples passed the time
renaming kinds of rubble. Instead of loss
they had dreaming. No heartbreak. For the length
of a cobbled day, whatever they saw in each other's gazes
dripped from the buildings as music.

·

A hinge turning in a stranger's life. A friend walking
toward you in a crowded room. A sound like a sketch.
A blank drawn. An awkward moment in conversation.
A letter in the mail. A mode of transport. A set
of excuses. A distance. A pain in your left temple.
A finite dream. A slip of the senses. A closed lid.
A garden fountain. A fear vector. A need
to be addressed. A need for sound. A brown lawn.
A sky littered with faded jet trails.

If it won't fit into words, we resort to song. Trying to
finish the cigarette slowly, hoping the bus won't arrive
on schedule. The trees are ashake with time.
Because the canopy blocks most of the sky, the street
corner feels like a living room. White lamps hang
from the lower branches. The cold of early spring
suddenly occupies our timeline. If it won't stay,
we claw at it, hoping something will linger. Behind
every stranger's face is this weary hope. I want to say,
"Look up." Or for the falling twigs to start emitting
notes upon impact. If things won't sparkle, retrain the eye.

•

Each morning we would walk through the dirt soccer
fields strewn with garbage. We wore our navy blue
school uniforms and kicked up dust. How my grandfather
shrank after the cancer took hold, I've always wondered.
If it penetrates you, if it plants the seed of death in your bones,
can you call this your body? Had I the words. Had I not been so
like a juncture, I might have spoken with him in more honest
ways. What can time do but pass? My mother would bring me
to his bedside every few days, like she wanted me to sense
the weight of it. Can you ride your bike now?
he would ask me. Do you still fall every time you stop?

•

It rained for four whole years. The crops gorged and drowned.
We drew portraits of the city. Our monuments,
half-hidden in clouds. Some banded together
for survival. Others wrote love letters to God.
God remained curious as a child. Much like today,
we pondered by windows. The pipes rusted.
What happened afterwards, I'm not quite sure.
We were to dream. A child told us, Go forth,
life is waiting at the bottom of the steps, to your left.
You will know it by its seriousness. Laugh.

In rest homes, patients hang on as if trying to commit
some sound to memory. The inverse shape
of what a life becomes. I, who've lived on the coast
for a decade plus, drink excess amounts of coffee and tea
to get through the morning. Small beachside towns
becoming homogenous. The stranded "I" watching
from the sidewalk, curious for a last form of listening.
Each day made of scrapped music. A pebble in fragments.
The space revealed by broken forms. In solitude
our hands grow brittle. Memories of touch
start to go.

.

She arrived with a hermit crab shell, small as a world,
in the palm of her calloused hand. As you grow older,
she told me, you will come to such sights,
by and by, and you won't know whether to weep
or harden. Years later, I sat on a park bench alone, looking
down at my fingers, the grassy knoll before me outlined
by the lights of the financial district. I remembered
there were no more wild tigers. I remembered stepping
forward, each with our own camera, our own flash
containing its negation like a coin.

.

To celebrate death we arrange the day's remnants
into loving patterns. To arrive at our own absence
we decide on a new name. To know its depth
we put on old gazes. To build a history we mind
our boundaries. To retrain the eye we close it.
To start again we make our way through mounds
of garbage. To hear its song we wait in stations.
To touch love's end we squander our lives.

Across the screen scroll today's top searches:
polar bears, egg recall list. I'm not waiting for my
body to dissolve, but only hoping that my eyes
will stop recognizing yellow. It's a strange world out there,
without our personal ways of remembering. I want to hear
this as song. The rioters hurling fire. Aren't we all
just doing our jobs? I want this wavelength carved. The sound
of fighter jets over the apartment. A place to live in
while the sun runs out of things to hammer
into grapes.

.

Limbs bursting through bolted doors. Limbs marching
through a crowded room. Limbs dancing to the pull
of unhinged minds. Limbs lying. Limbs contracting
in pleasure. Limbs with newspapers. Limbs
at the border between madness and boredom.
Limbs free from thirst. Limbs falling out of broken time
slots. Limbs seated in neat, cushioned rows. Mute
limbs. Limbs moving in tandem with the ground's
vibrations. Limbs discarded on a Sunday morning. Limbs
meeting silently for dinner.

.

And we divided the world into purchasable pieces.
Billboards apologize simply by winking. It's a good night
if we stumble home unbroken. A good night if the pack
rips at the carcass. Could you pass the salt? she says.
Could you be the one who stays? We pretend to know.
At the bottom of those thoughts we have no
tongue for, in that place where silence and sight
intersect, we stand on one foot, swaying in a fog.
When both our silent chests sway in tandem,
we call this dancing. As in, we sat at the coffee table,
dancing. Or, it was easy to ignore the stop signs
as we laughed all the way to Moscow, dancing.

Each pebble in the stream lends its shape
to the water's flow. The river ahead
carries these small dances in its threads.
The symphony wants to survive, does sometimes
in the form of nostalgia. I cried
and it seemed the least sentimental thing to do. This
notion of days as patches of insight and loss,
a kind of open loneliness. A muralist finding his paint. Diving
past the wall to the place where his figures go on floating.

.

In paradise the flags are sleeping, fading in the rivers
without hurry. All names are blood memory.
The heart blooming is also the sound of leaves burning.
Knotted strings litter the gardens. Each word
has its tiny ghost. When I look up
the window is open. The cold in the room fills my eyes.
The broken radio patiently gathers history. Atop my
desk sits a glass of cold tea. A ray of red traffic light touches
the sill. I can hear the young couple on the floor above
promising never to fight again.

.

To wake from the portrait, scream. Or to wake
from the portrait, touch the tip of your tongue
to the roof of your mouth. To process the sound
of separation, walk far into the crowd. To move
in fault lines, to keep from starving, we talk about it.
To step forward, to balance on the string, knotted
at points, to propel the thing unsaid through locks
and chain, to keep our hands from breaking, our judgment
from aging, we skip waking, eyes weightless

I threw my bag into the stranger's car and got in.
I hid my altered state by nodding in a serious manner.
I listened to his long sentences that fell about
in all directions. I looked past the glass, at the mountain range.
At the clouds lowering themselves
onto the slopes. At the clouds beginning to roll
into the valley. I concealed my worry by periodically
refocusing my eyes. I leaned my head against the window
when I ran out of questions, hummed in my head
a line of anxious music.

.

Whole cities have sprouted from weariness. In a land
far away, people commute and cook dinner in fear
that a pop song will toss them toward the sky. A rapture
marked by leftover pavement. And what about the war?
I sit in the shop, letting the night go in peace. Basic
diplomacy. Looking at pictures. Trying to make out
what is actually there. Preparing to live with less space.
Retracting my tendrils. Remembering my spot on the map.

.

Inside the dead tree, the children built a fire
and tried to find the birthplace of each flame. Their hearts
drifted like ghosts. The flames rose from the small
pit of coal and dry newspaper, reached a peak and
vanished. The result was a kind of trance. The spastic
flashes colored the walls of the trunk and lent
the children's skins an ancient glow. The children smiled
as if this proved they still knew something. After a while
any constant noise can substitute for silence. When the flames
dimmed and the crackle subsided, there was the forest's
sighs and creaks.

Every day we obsessed over the outlines of our shells. The extent
to which love could confound us. We knew almost nothing
about the backs of our hands. We knew the uncomfortable
corners of the city. Wires nesting behind cardboard panels.
We knew how to stand outside government buildings
and how to fall asleep anywhere. We rode in packed cars.
Assumed we would eventually grow out of it. We drew
maps of famous graves to follow. Claimed the dead air
for our own. We knew it was best to leave unfinished.
To go back and risk ordinary lives.

·

No one goes into a cave lightly, even to hide. Mighty
are the numbers drifting out there. Try turning off the lights
and paint what you remember. Paint the wall of screens
that caught you. The way hands hold still. The blue glow
of the sand during red tides. What remains are not stories
but moments of color that stain. The song
from the speakers drifting to the window and fading
down into the sidewalk full of plans. We would often lie
on the grass, waiting. I'd leave my hand
on her waist for hours, attempting to record.

·

It's true that the gods may discard their shapes.
They do it often, in a place of complete peace where
the problems of humans cannot move them. Our language
cannot concern them. They are not open to structures
or prayer. What they like to see is light shows. Bodies
on stages, plumed and wild, propelled by the fear
of inertia. They like bodies thrown in spectacle,
torn at the hinges, hearts expunged, ghosts expelled
in moments of white. The spark of leaving. The sound
of our fabric undone.

Is it possible to get rid of time by refusing
to make machines? Packing all one's life in a suitcase,
and disappearing into the white room
where we sat and built a fire
and had no patience for melody. The edges held no shimmer.
The sound of the paper did not make us dream. And so
we ate it. And grew obsessed.
With endings. With the perimeter of bells. With screens.
My friends slept on the floor and one day the floor
gave out beneath them, and they let go their thin phones
in the quick strum of the fall.

.

Before they wake. Before the scraps of vision
have been turned into wallpaper. A vehicle the size
of invention, sputtering. Or films.
And some language, where the shadows of raindrops
on windows   Or a feeling. Drain
pipes dangling free in the wet curve of the alley.
Skies full of old motion. We are told to fear strangers
for they are points of absolute uncertainty.
Told to be faithful as if time did not exist.

.

One man says to another, do you see my colors?
I've worked hard for these matching eyes. One man
watches a crowd in silence. One man's wife
stops acknowledging his body, going about as usual
in a different time. One man waits for a scene to repeat.
One man dedicates his free time to erasing, usually two
hours after work, before going to bed. One man admires
photographs all night. One sits on the wet earth
and starts eating the strawberries.

Our skin thickens, and it's now possible
to change its color. My dream is to one day
have a counter, over which I'll toss back and forth
some whims that I've collected. Like the notion
that Storyville is brutal. That I will always
be searching for a kind of meeting ground.
The yellow lamp we got for the desk is a
basic luxury. Tonight we fear all the right joys.
For your birthday I will buy you any ideology
you want, or that batch of wispy clouds that resemble stretch-
marks.

·

A word meaning intentional disclosure of a private
history. A word that resembles an iceberg. A word meaning
accidental nights. A word hiding in noise. A word meaning
to wake to the sound of a roommate's cough. A word
that mimics refraction. A word for when shadows do not
match their objects. A word receding. A word arriving at the shore.
A word hiding behind a black mustache. A word meaning
a place one decides to forget. A word meaning the textures
of silences.

·

Matamoros will always be gray. Soft ash of factories
covering streets and sky. I see myself walking by a pack
of stray dogs lounging in the wooden porch of a tiny
corner store. Walls covered with rusted brand names.
Aluminum ads nailed to the door. Prices jutting
from dusty shelves. The occasional gunshot, far away,
not to be worried over. It's all more dream than memory.
The way we patch our cities together from bits of sound
and leftover light, basing the self on compiled
suspicions. To honor some original gesture
that might or might not have been.

Plastic blue seats of the bus full of dirt crumbs
and skin flakes. On some days the view of the ocean
fails to displace the nausea. Visual show of bravery
meaning not enough. Attempts recorded and made
objects. There must be easier ways of doing this. They
say fear lifts the coma. But we don't quite fear,
not while sitting by the whir of the engine. Every day
staring at that same ocean for as long as we can bear.
Sometimes we learn to ignore its sound. Even so,
it becomes eventually part of our gestures, part
of the way we hit the pavement and disperse.

.

No blame was ascribed to the slaughter, which was
judged to be "necessary" and "proportional."
We can't deny a killer his artistry.
Watching ourselves twist.
Observing from a cluster. Special lights for washing
our pores away. We will never know the color
of our skin, which was, after all, the desired effect.
A PR victory, a painted path. The way cadets
step into assigned footprints made of yellow
like homesickness.

.

Growing displaced. Pressing buttons at crossings.
Passing by epicenters, the clouds slow and archaic.
In any one of these three-bedroom homes, a push
and pull could be afoot. The fight to keep momentum going.
A can of iced tea in the manicured yard. Framed days,
geometry's innocence. The touch of familiar music.
Say no to silence. Say no in an empty canyon. Remember
trash days. Rules of engagement. Pain's due.

It became fashionable to fall on swords. Every day,
we fell on any and all swords we could find.
If you came across a sword in public, this was ideal. Even more
so if you knew how to fall with appropriate flare and
more so if you fell with the right people watching.
It all ended of course when the swords rusted and dulled.
No one knew how to make any more of them. Nostalgic
revival attempts lasted for weeks. There was no
traditional sense. We enjoyed walking across bridges
in the cold. Failure was simple and easy.

.

Trash collector walks down the aisle, bag in hand, examining
each point of concentrated light before tossing it.
The clouds below are herd-like. The wings of the plane are
patched metal. This chamber, with its sleeping heads, can be
seen from the ground, with a squint. The children in the backseats
cry because of air caught in their ears.
Make up dreams for the sleepers. Let shapes drift
into some realm where you might find people you loved
trying to mean again. High up here, the blunders we caused
below seem cold and obvious. That we now arrive at the clouds
on a regular basis fails to ease any fears.

.

We misspeak. I meant I liked you. I had the best
of nouns in mind. I meant to pay more attention.
The wind always makes its way in somehow. We see it
as romantic or laughable, depending. "How terrifying
that words can almost mean." Darling, we say,
ephemera. I have a black pen for making labyrinths. God
forbid this become more interesting than silence.
This morning began as always: trying to recall why I wanted
to get up early. Trying to remember that a heart can give out
at the sudden experience of structure. That belief is lustful
and eager and curious before beauty. That you can hear its
whisper in the tempered dark.

And if words were to split open and flower, and if
the days were sleeping there, and if the mind were to falter
carefully, aiming its fall, landing at the center of this
ocean, and if she suddenly gave you her clothes, and if angels
agreed to sit and discuss the uncertain future of our country,
and say you longed to be absent of feeling, and say numb
inner chambers exist, and if duplicate deaths became
the fashion, and if the sun beat heavy on your tired feet,
and what if you heard it as news, and if the air around you
were to suddenly acquire color, and if a click could paste
your dream elsewhere, and if your shell were but thinly attached
to the outside.

When the dog catches the cat and doesn't know
what to do, what do they do? Do they dance? It's an odd
thing to witness. Makes one turn away almost
instantly. Not repulsed but shaken. A need
for something solid, even ritual, arises. What dream
could it be, behind the stage flooded with laughter?
                              For your birthday
I will draw you a map to the clearing that was promised
in our early days. There you can shed your name.
In the evenings watch the fireflies bicker
between the branches.

                    .

I'm trying my best to retain the good parts
of our long-ago drive to the coast, entranced as I am
by these streets full of windows. Even as the redwoods
begin and the road curves beyond sight,
I keep picturing a nation full of sad affairs, its comical death
keeping you warm for as long as it takes to repair your radio.
It's nearly summer and the trees along the boardwalk
just west of our apartment form a grotesque menagerie.
None of them are from here, this remodeled land.

                    .

Each sweater has its tiny ghost. She leaves my red
tie on the armoire handle. For the rest of the day we are free
to waste our time redefining phrases. For it's illegal
to destroy these phrases. For we built lives there. And so
we go to the mountains if we want to discard all possible
meanings. The trees can hide us for a while.
Faces sleeping in the afternoon. Threads of fabric
adjusting to the shape of our limbs.

Build me a beast half as brave as returning
without objects. If love is armor and if love
is the naked face, notice how people idle around a sculpture
in their own particular ways. If the concrete were to bloom
the people's idle ways would shatter.
In my free time I dream of engines
that run on nightfall. Of shelters we can carry
in our pockets. The thing is to keep building
even as skin flakes off our hands. Even as the notions
that kept us awake for hours listening to ourselves think
seep into the colors of the room.

.

What we kept was a childish love of throwing stones
into deep empty places and listening. We used to wait sometimes
for days before the first sounds reached us, watching the moss
gather on the stones we sat on, feeling ourselves feeling
what we knew to be summer, in our thin clothes,
looking up at the clouds full of old-world patience.
And we had a vague notion of what patience entailed. Time
stretched itself to accommodate our brand new minds.
We'd lie side by side, under the bed, telling ghost stories,
hoping the other would be brave enough this time
to reach over and touch an exposed waist.

.

I still wish I could write dreams into your nerves so that when
you next blink words mean their musicality. I stared at the
dusty rim of the glass and thought of my grandmother
with her lonely face, climbing wooden ladders in the sierras
and tending her chickens. This is where the breeze feels
like the sky reaching down to him, and the child learns
something about the size of people, our constantly
shifting shapes. The eyes of the old woman covered
in cloudy membrane. Her laughter full of many days gone.

Before it's over, you're allowed to steal an interaction.
To say goodbye to a friend as she walks out the door,
drops her keys, reaches down for them. Her glasses
sliding off, hitting the tile and shattering. To see her die
in the collective dream. To bear witness as she stops providing
data. That I can tie you down and undo your buttons,
that you can dismiss me with a simple sound. That we've arrived
at this laminate floor, somehow conflicted over the nature
of unicorns. Whether we'd been better off without them.
How their pupils change when they see the sunrise.
Whether their horns bleed.

.

Can we help that our hearts might've at last
been abstracted from the universe of things? Will this
new touchscreen let me hide my body? Our due
has come if we still care for it. Light as it travels to all
the dark places. Here in my corner office, I remain human
as best I can. The whir of the towers continues unremarkable.
I cannot complain about my back in this ergonomic chair,
I tell myself to pass the time. The fault is in my posture.
I can only look at those less fortunate than me, those with
rigid chairs and non-adjustable heights.

.

Step 1: I'm floating through noon in a midsized city,
all part failure and all elemental parts. A collage of table décor
plastered on a boutique window anchors the scene. Around it
the joints on the sidewalk swerve. Elegant bi-pedal successes
heading for safety. Between the recognized patterns there is,
on occasion, the residue of plants. Drinking tea
and thinking of the ways we're put together. I'm sorry
I've been ambivalent lately. The city looks better at night
and everyone acts accordingly, giving way to the latest
form of what can be called living.

The time when men felt inferior to nature
might have passed. But this cannot be a beginning.
Things that ring in our inner ears like star-bursts
are hard to trust, for they move our insides
without our say-so. Why is it that, sitting at the foot
of the sea cliffs, with only the ocean before me, I am
more aware of the plaster buildings half a mile inland?
Each room has a different way of returning sound.
The rumbling of traffic emanates from the carpet's hairs.
We visit each other as the nights grow shorter, forced
to find common ground from shared uncertainty.

·

We experience our losses in increments of waking.
I would like a natural experiment to fondle
our little nostalgic minds. I would like my heart
in a thousand small jars. I was always a bit embarrassed
at my lack of words. The seagulls in their whiteness
seemed wild and humiliating. I talked to a stranger
when I grew tired of my familiar parts, careless, sparking
with curiosity. I stepped into the untried mistakes knowing
nothing. The idea was to reach into God's bowels
and see how we fared in the years that followed.

·

I'm hungry. I'm tired. I'm going to build my towers here,
from memory, on brittle ground. I saw it on television.
I regret too many things to regret more. I'm broke. I'm re-
fracturing my fingers so they can be set properly this time.
I'm a small body with a ranging stare. I'm unemployed. I'm a
mirror of the people who taught me to string together
meaning and sound. I have a country to run. I'm going
to play this "as if." And while the armies are away,
I'll stay and keep the orphanage clean, and the flower fields
stocked with breezes scrolled off the sea.

Our refusal to make machines will result in inconveniences
and rediscovery. I've been obsessed with winged bugs
ever since I walked through the tiny coastal town that
leisured in the sun each morning, keeping its people
tan and comfortably productive. It's a land
of hummingbirds above bushes in the gardens of
retirement homes. On the small pier, a gaunt pilgrim
waits for sunset, eyes closed, taking in the sludge of information
seeping through the air. Knowing there's no rescuing
yesterday's mind. That we must choose to remember each day
why we love our memories, or if.

·

The subject is lost. Erased. The subject is wedged
between fashion lines. The subject is unspeakable, blue and
full of winds. The subject, meaning the stem, the instant of
detachment, the moment of sudden, un-retractable freedom. To float.
To be caught by the hungry. The subject is a network of foreign
veins, full of rooms and the irrational impulse to survive.
The subject, alone, deciding the time and place of its
emergence. The subject, deciding nothing. The subject arriving
at its own still image, being worn and used by a few
and slipping smoothly through the rest.

·

This is exactly the problem. It all happens when no one
is looking. And no one is looking. And this is the solution
too? In the café, there is a woman alone with her laptop and a
sticker. "I was there," we declare. We matter. A glass of red
covered with a cloth napkin sits atop her table. Speakers
blare out used couplets. It's 8:23 PM and I'm trying to
remember why I shouldn't sleep. The helicopters float
above the city like candelabra. All night we look for crawlspaces
where for the length of a few whispers we can take
our clothes off and celebrate our warm decay.

And the song that made you cry comes on as you drink
your first coffee and wait out your last few hours
in this city that raised you. Your looks are
laughable and you're my favorite epigraph of the artist's world.
And you're leaving now. Getting on a plane
and leaving, and your friends will miss you. And everything
will be different and the same. And you don't yet know
all the ways of remaining alive. And you won't ever.
And the song stops. The silenced music has opened up
the room's murmur, the television mounted on the wall
announcing the things we can expect to happen next.

.

Our methods were savage and unrefined. Every song opened up
as we touched its underside with hindsight. There, we made
our first homes. With blunt objects and a sense of the years
as immeasurable, we cobbled together plans
upon plans, and just the barest of shelters. We put up
our antennas and called out for interference. In a broken treehouse,
my friend and I shared an apple, and we shared what we had left
of our open-ended dream. We talked about hunger and said that yes,
we did someday want to learn the flowers. The ladder
that led down to the forest floor was loose and splintered,
so we held on to the brittle rope of the tire swing.

.

In their small perforated rooms, the refugees scan the air
for intelligible sound. A fragment of a jingle or a token
forecast of tomorrow's winds. A shot of a woman
gathering her dead from empty malls. All through the cities
our lovely computers crawl the leftovers
for useful stats: evidence. That we tried at least
to direct our shrapnel. That it was never meant to go
too long into the night. The singer sat atop the sea cliffs
one evening with his friends, who held up their drinks
and yelled at the planes that the world was the size
of their voices.

If you enjoyed the pipe dream, you might also like old
rumpled sheet music. If you enjoyed the heavy air of your
childhood farm, you might also like these haunted castles
full of ivy. If you are lost in the forest, this tiny bell
will keep your memories till you find inner peace and no
longer need them. If you liked the slow sex of winter, you will
love these dead flags flapping in the sunset. If the roar
of the last few tigers kept you awake, you might enjoy this new
coat of red feathers. If you keep falling through the floor
during sleep, it might be the perfect time to count your losses
and learn their names. If you enjoyed the splatter effects of our
latest war, you may take a stranger's hand and step outside.

                                    .

Denied or not, the logic of mistakes rings
like a bell in clear air each time. With its complex
fictions, it moves our choices this way and that,
and we sense it in the crosswalks of the city,
in the eyes of all the readers of centuries-old books
that propel their authors' minds along thin threads
into the present cluster of millennial hearts. With our
grownup names and mixed drinks, we linger under the
light of screens and wait for earthrise. The cold liquid
runs its course slowly. We feel it pause between our
lungs like a tourist. Its sound, we imagine, is a silver
ping.

                                    .

We abstained from celebrating birthdays and the holidays
for years under the banner of a strange religion. And when
my mother learned that we could not, under this faith, give our
blood, we stopped attending services and singing for God.
Our elders were dying and blood was all we had
to give them. Blood was where we kept our memories,
and dominion of our blood was birthright. My mother who
taught me the letters and the various ways they lie, in our first
cinderblock home, working and playing and waiting
for better news.

That was sad but fun. The skeleton inside you
rusts slowly, and you stop at the
intersection to record the feeling. What now?
Some people spend their allotted time
redecorating the landscape. Some people talk at each other
for comfort, some crisscross a room or an empty
beach. We keep our glances away from each other
and focus on the waves. The kindness of looking
away from the broken parts that hint at something
broken. All the habits that stayed.

.

When the methods of transmission are as complex
as the message. When everything's replaced by image.
When we bow in a general direction. When our
tendency to flourish as we rot quickens. We tense.
We chose to either let imagination loose or not.
We step into the clothes of a flawed stranger sitting
in a bar full of sports fans, attempting to meditate while
carving his likeness into the face of a wooden statuette.
An enforced loneliness called rebirth, or transcendence,
or a kind of reconciliation with the objects that remember us.
This morning we woke up naked. Our bodies
stood in sunlight with their fragile portals.

.

In a faraway regime, new radicals stand on rooftops
and signal to each other with colorful scarves. From the air
the drones capture the rustle of cloth that covers
the country. Is this the genesis of art? Not revolution
but a need for solace? Windows lit up in the night. Smog
giving way to layered darkness so that wanderers can find
a way through splintered alleys that hide off the roads.
This land is not our land or yours. Here
the repercussions of not speaking in code are real.
The true meaning of each word hangs from the underside
of its sound, like an iron weight threatening to sink it.

Do I sit before the question now or later? Do I keep
its ring inside my hat? Do summers go by faster
when you're moving every day to new houses and each
newsbreak follows you from room to room until
it's fall and the radio has lost track of its intentions?
Should I wait by the door, or in the yard where you can see me?
Do I make myself, in your eyes, clear? Do I include
the nervous tick? Can we edit that out? Can we
pretend I'm the same person as the one in my profile
picture? Do we have that kind of time? As we look down
to watch the skyline moving, could you hold

.

The shapes I move inside have started to become
attached. Like how heat blasts melt the victims' clothes
onto their skins   but far away
I slipped as I went up the stairs and missed the sunset
coming through my window. I heard the empty house
echo, as signals began to fail and my human parts
started spilling out one by one. The memories of my
first country unhooked and floated up into the already
cluttered sky. Me as an old man over and over.
Waking each morning and writing notes on my arm
to have the feeling of flesh in motion.

.

If we could just take back the buildings and their shadows.
We didn't know this was going to happen,
we say aloud. We will put away the icons and subsequent
elegies and from now on be humble. But we all know
something we keep to ourselves. We wonder in public
about the moon and in our rooms stay silent. If you come by
tonight, I only ask that you don't worry about manners
and forget the arrangements of heavenly bodies. Leave
the lonely parts on the steps. There's no room on the table.
What enters here must be agile, simple, free.

I am waiting in the kitchen for her to put on clothes
and find her purse. Waiting for her to come downstairs
and begin the day. She's taking her time, because it's
hers and I should know this. After dropping her off
at the station, the afternoon fills with all the familiar turns.
Traffic flow. Amusement booths that simulate a hurricane,
$2. And now the day is about waiting for the night in some
worthy way. Hatching strategies to mold instinct
into evening. Trying to give the evening weight enough to fall
through our distractions and land in the place where memories
cycle. "Don't focus on the finger," she tells me, "or you'll miss
the heavenly glory."

.

The symphony lifts you up, out of the city, and never
drops you in the same place it found you,
but lower down, somewhere deep and unfinished.
Follow the lights to readjust your senses. Turning
the nearest doorknob for the sake of touch, we are again
confronted with the lights of storefronts flickering.
Alive again at night, small in the full-throttle sound
of our machines. All the familiar urges: dreams and
cave paintings fed back to us. Bipedal success bumping
into unexpected meetings on its way to safety. Billions
of small delays streaming down. Voices filtered. Signals
rising out of speakers into crowded eyes.

.

Figments   apertures   smallness
        infractions   Under the desert   Here we make
our home   skylights   In sleep   skipping
our eyes again   These clouding   Falling out
            bursting through   one   the other   shift of
        Rain   at rest
the very least   each drop's descent
    Slanted for   strict effect
pleasure taken   Inside water   we talk
    how the landing will   assuming the best
    Almost   that things don't end   clockwork

Waiting for the train again. Reading about delicate men
in positions of power. White floor tiles reflecting bright
ceiling lights. It's Sunday. At last night's gathering, I watched
everyone's faces shifting from one expression to the next.
There was little to say. Today's news involves a closer look
at the ancient chitchat covering the walls of Pompeii.
Outside, a protest continues its march to the college. Let's
count all the things we've added and say: Did we fail these
spaces? We filled the valley with music. We spread our astounding
irrelevance. Tossed our maps of home to the ground.
And now we smile over glasses of wine. We languish in love
and lean against windows, dreaming of arrival.

·

I had a kid-sized version of my father's rocking chair.
Had wide open days I spent tearing off flakes of shale
from the cliff next to our house. I tricycled down slopes, scraped
my arms. I was chased by street dogs for having thrown flakes
of shale at them. Thinking but not having the words
to speak of the feeling of smallness. The earth's architecture
seemed to care nothing for ours. I've almost forgotten it now
as I exit into the morning on cold days, exhale and stare
at my breath, go for the car keys and try out a line from a good
movie to test its ring: "I've been dead for years. But so much
of me still lives in the places where I stopped to look around."

·

Some of them refused to live their days at gunpoint.
Some were shot repeatedly. Now, which is the
fastest way to the ocean? The effect of grandiose vision is that
everywhere becomes a potential stage, and nothing is left
but stage props. "Take my picture." I hear it's okay to drive
by the tamed tigers. What solid thing is there to hold? "O
to arrive at youngness and discover at last the secret of age."
But I'm not there yet. I'm here, in these condensed days,
teaching privileged kids to avoid fragments. 2:55 PM.
Counting corpses again. Strings of robberies. Animals found
who were trying to leave.

We bought postcards. I stood with the others
in the airport terminal, watching through the window
as our plane docked. The same scenes played over
in our minds. That we are all strangers is our common ground.
This is the way we agree to politely tread. Well then.
Someone snaps a picture on their phone. A group of children
ignore me. They climb onto the nearby seats and put their palms
against the window panes. Outside, the cargo compartment
has opened. Our selected possessions thrown inside.

.

Dear mind, I'm leaving now, I hope this letter finds you.
Dear stranger, whatever weight you have to give my words,
I'll take it gladly to the hill behind the house where we made
a small pyre. Dear driftwood, the edge is coming.
The planks of my raft have started to soften. Dear
tote bag, the things spilling from your ruptured seams
onto the floor, what a world. Dear men and women who dally
in the starlight, your eyes already old-fashioned. Dear iris,
flourish. Dear drip of centuries-old words, your black
surfaces must break to let out the sounds and colors. Dear
dying pride, today I wandered out on foot, saw the temples
and the strongholds and the sphinxes that you left.

Standing over the well, he tries to picture the stones
he has thrown into the dark. Their impacts bounce up
from wall to wall, out into the open air where his ears wait.
When the villagers walk by and see him there
alone in the clearing, leaning forward, gaze fixed
on the spot where the earth has opened,
some put down their loads and watch for a minute
while they rest. Those who venture to ask why he's there
are always given the same answer. I once had a field of dandelions,
he tells them. And then centuries of human death fell upon it.
It was next to this big green sea, where the severed head of Orpheus
floated by each morning with its song.

.

After all the twisted journeys, I stepped through a narrow
door on the side of a tiny building. There's no getting
out alive. I'm just looking for a place to enjoy
the earned bruises. I've ended up with these
dreams made of dreams made of still frames. Marie
used to like lying naked, face down on the bed
with the windows open, happy in her body
and the safety of a room. The search for a new place
to be vulnerable has proven rough and speckled with years.
Every day the planes fly between the tops of buildings.
Through her window she sees the vast open spaces
above the houses, hears the roar of engines gliding down.

.

It's been the coldest summer yet. People in cafés
with laptops looking for jobs. Fog clinging to the hills
in the afternoon. Cats staring out of street-side windows
then crawling out of sight with indifferent grace. The wind
sweeping the canyons of downtown. An aged woman,
grown hard but with a kernel of fragility that she keeps
secret, picking out bottles from the trash. A red leaf blows
in from the sidewalk and settles on the hardwood floor
of a sandwich shop. Lights turn green. A handful of lives
go by. A pause, a noise, something on plasma.

Must we divide the length of our residence into such
tiny hours? Hours we blink through while trying to hold
the hand of any stranger who will look us in the eye and stay? This
vice of constantly recording the impossible precision of trees,
the impulsive adding of our breath to the winds that keep
the dust afloat. Sometimes it makes sense to just sit in the sand
and watch. To forget about shame and the rules that it stands on.
You'll know the terror of freedom by the way it keeps the center
of your guts awake as the rest of you drifts.

.

Three doves fly across the intersection. A wind brushes our
hands as we wait for the next overdue earthquake. Our planes,
which rise from our perfect asphalt, today will take us anywhere
for the perfect photograph of skies over landmarks. The bus
arrives on schedule. I open my wallet, see my picture. Our days
held in sustainable patterns. I know the streets here
but the lives contained in each building I pass stay imagined,
fed by small glimpses into windows and exclamations
overheard. Then this nervous shaking of my foot as I sit
at my table and contemplate the shapes in the room.
The echo of wings settles in my ear like a reminder
of what I can't know.

.

Everything I wagered would last, I placed in the suitcase.
Everything I wagered would last at least until my
fortunes were again proved wrong. Most photographs
I took for the purpose of breaking my own heart later.
The convoys that passed us on our way to the border
were full of armored faces. There were eyes
behind glass and machine guns held in relaxed fashion.
Smile and wave to the feeling of impermanence.
Halfway through the drive we turned the steering wheel inland
to see where a strange dirt path led.

His favorites were the weeds in late December covered in frost.
He walked by them on his way to school each morning.
That all of us shiver in endlessness was a sort of comfort. That we
die in these moments that stay in someone else's stash.
Even if our exhalations enter the air without us. He knew
none of it in words. Only that windstorms occasionally came
and sent empty cans and paper trash bags flying over him. Only
that he sometimes sat and watched the old man floating in his sea
of final seconds. Sitting there he could sometimes imagine
how the decades would happen. Wondered how he too
would see his world replaced.

.

What a thing to be standing
at the edge of anywhere, again beginners. Taking stock
of our body's new language. The urge to outlive our fathers,
forcing us to move. Planted in this landscape of glitches
and wrong directions. Young men waiting at the foot of iron balconies
for a scene that won't repeat. Keeping track of the moon.
The opening and closing of the flowers. Satellites turning
beyond layers of cloud. Under all of it, I lie prostrate,
tossing my vocabulary piece by piece till some word catches
on a hand.

.

Answers were a matter of spiderwebs. If any perspective
is possible, then let me see me through your shellshock days,
your boredom or your empty hands. My curiosity swelled
as it was left to wander in the hallways of the Palace of Fine Arts
where I first learned to take what wasn't mine or of
my station. To not limit one's capacity to break things is
what I meant to re-enact. But a hole is hidden at the bottom
of our best intentions. What doesn't float falls straight through.
Empty cars left in the sun. Signs that once hung from rusted wire.
Us and our neighbors in our painted rooms.

By means of murmuring, I gave rhythm to my mornings
in near silence, mouthing syllables as the ocean passed by
outside, wild even through the scratched plastic windows
of the bus. Strangers slept in the seats beside me. Men with
dark leathered skin like my father's. Green stains on their jeans
from yard work. Old women talking of the war. I sat beside them,
thinking my music, all of us moving down the coast,
some of us watching the swallows and seagulls suspended
over the waves outside by means of non-resistance. Then the bus
stopping and the birds passing from sight.

·

Today is the start of a world that can hold you for the waking
hours that are left. Here, in the playground of a sleeping head,
a city of replayed meetings flowers like a new stranger
looking up and saying
     Where was I? I was watching the houses fragment
into endless iterations of themselves. The tragedy of love
always saying its intentions aloud until it means
a postcard. Nothing like the land where you were first
alive.

·

From one machine's belly to the next. Stepping through doors,
feeling expected. And thin. As wire. As windows speeding
past houses remind you that everything turns. Time and
hands clutching at lost insights. Drifting in stations,
numbers glowing red above our heads. I turn to the woman
on my left who's wearing headphones. I turn to the metal clatter
of the tracks and the glass doors hissing. Feeling
kinship with this mob of aging strangers. Self-made
like bad actors, fashioning ourselves onto the stage,
the props' pasts dissolving as we reach for them.

The general sense is that we hold a fortune in outdated
currency. We stand with our hands exposed. Wander around
in borrowed hats. When dinner is finished, I look up
from the paper and find myself grounded in the land of plenty
with no way of explaining why I need to leave. What
happens to untended stories? The last time I sat by the water
was a year ago, and we were about to never see each other again
for a while. I used all the words I could think of to make the sky
stop, but I had no clean sources to guide me. Somewhere,
in another dream maybe, our perceptions are grafted together
and we can feel the other floating elsewhere through the day.

·

One of the neighborhood sports was hunting lizards.
We made slingshots by hand and ran the muddy streets
in packs, screaming. We knew, in our way,
that our noises held little weight. That such weightlessness
had value never crossed our minds. We were nothing but a cluster
of loud blurs passing. Ignorance and hunger moved us like
engines. The lizards scattered in all directions. We picked up
pebbles and imagined everything, assuming that somewhere
somehow, anything could fly. We got stuck on barbed wire fences,
arrived home bloody and sweating, but sensing no death
in us yet.

·

Let playing be logical then, since the orders are sent and
our missiles linger in transit. Waiting is all this is, and up there
the sun hammers down human attempts to see. Our myths,
grown bare, lie flat at our feet.
                    Let playing be waking.
And what about all these mountains of ink?
         irony   goodbye   flowers
The petals were split, atom by atom
and we frolicked in the thin fire, and all the children
laughed under the stairs. Above us the sky, happily failing.
Language attempting to capture the pieces of blue in its net.

because it's strange to be alive on earth   because we passed
each other in a room full of pleasure unused because day
after day we wait by the stage because birds are discarding
their feathers in the sea because frames and shutters
pass from hands because storms and calms are swerving
because I can touch the surface of a loved one's picture
and make it recede because we played cards silently on
rainy days and stood on cliffs watching the helicopters drift
beneath the clouds

.

The ornament twirled and shattered. The world inside fell
into the hands of men. The hands fumbled. The world
again fell, this time landing at the edge of a lake. The reflection
it saw was unlike anything it had suspected. A new
taste crept into the dirt. Seizing the machines of men, the world
set once again to work. Let's yield to their hunger, said the leaves.
Let's watch the equation unfold. Let them play out their myth
of beautiful insanity. And we sat for a while on the patio,
reading the news. Feeling the numbers moving in the wind.
Bookshelves sinking. Our common hearts falling barely
out of reach. And we had, still, these tender partings, laid out so
gently, as if made of more than just lives and their endings.

.

Like a pencil dropped from a tenement rooftop,
falling slowly past windows, almost motionless,
outside of time, where it's cold, landing on the asphalt,
thin and yellow, too light to have broken, an object
in a landscape again.
          Like dangling your legs over the edge of a cliff,
suddenly sprouting wings and having options.   Like cotton
brushing against skin that has been sweating for hours,
filling with moisture.
          Like a white dress hanging in the closet, waiting
for a body to animate its folds, an occasion that will warrant
again its plain bareness.

We unbuttoned our clothes and fucked behind the stone
mausoleum, her hands against the cold wall, the hills around us
descending in folds of grass and curving walkways and two hundred
years of graves. Far away, the city at midday in autumn
looked faded in the sun. We breathed in small
rhythmic gasps. Pushed ourselves out into the surface
of our skins. The way exposure made them new, allowing us to live
in the delight of strewn garments. In the almost silence
of the hollow air, the almost silence in which all the small collisions
moving in us like an ocean   could be heard.

·

In the blank space
                              Our cellphones opened and
Saw the message, something about long lines
                              of icebergs
       Moving in patterns. Planning in tandem
              With the impacts and deflections
of a world of waves. Tonight in the yard, reading
       by screenlight.   The sound of talk
and wine   an owl's cry
What I meant to remember, there
          the white moment, the smell of dark hair
Under a moon
                              Perfectly halved

·

Our memories got cold and hardened. These
are my hands aging, we realized.
       This is the shape of oil in water. The same
scenes begin to loop in your head just before the big
decision.
       The forest looks black and alive from the seat
of the airplane. Here is how we fall from the sky in
comfort. The story of love saved in files. We scroll
through our pictures during landing. Study the faces
of people we know. Are told to be seated, stay calm.

The girl arrived in a torn dress and sat in the sand,
leaned back and rested her weight on her elbows.
I was just standing in this crowded subway car, startled,
thinking of your photograph. The way your hair was
caught just so, in the process of branding itself in my unused
memory. How strange to have this new set of keys.
We walked back, after our failures, to the rooms we were still
allowed to enter. There we aged, sleeping in arms, under the sound
of traffic and distant music. The red tide glowed fluorescent
and I read in my dreams under its light, about worlds
of confused workers. The nagging feeling that we've lost
the tiny details of our best affairs.

.

And men keep the world compartmentalized in their minds
as in a house of drawers and each day they pull one out
and study the thing inside for centuries. And women walk around
in sparks of synaptic arms that reach for all seas at once.
And men inscribe their names in glass and women pour wine.
And men leaf through pages looking for pictures of their first home
and women collect books in the empire's green ruins. And men
sit by windows in December watching the colors in the sky. And
women step through doors contemplating ways of exiting
other lives. And men run their fingers along the veins on the backs
of their hands. And women brush away strands of hair.

.

From steel rooms, we kept the cities optimized.
In the hot evenings of September, I sat in bed, my back
against the window, the music from the basement
feeding the walls. Our ceiling white and peeling. Each year
we grow more attached to the things we think we've earned.
The day-and-night sound of cars fades in and out of earshot.
And we're standing on concrete, waiting for a signal
to appear before our eyes. The sudden slowing
of a random moment making us see. People growing past
and leaving. Some of us at tables, studying our accidents.
Parts of our lives beginning to resemble paper boats.

The old man waited for his wife to die, between the orange
groves and the flat skies, for years. The tongues of his shoes
worn by the sun and the rain that sometimes fell. I'm sorry
I can't tell you of the amplified sound of my veins,
is what she thought of telling him, but she had only strength
to suck softly on the fruits he brought each morning. As much as I try,
I can't imagine sitting as he did, so close to her day after day.
Her eyes almost always closed. No noise at all in the afternoons
except the occasional goat, or the wind going by.
The empty room afterwards.

.

The spectator is not lost but cracked open,
looking out as the sounds of the city fall into him
in faded waves. The paint on the doors ages
while in the streets our fellow residents hurry
for shelter. Afraid of what they might see of their hearts
in the naked vista, they refuse to pause. I have no idea what he's
waiting for. In everyone else, there's an urge to continue marching.
But we all feel at least some of this odd restraint, almost a fear
of pushing the decade along. Everyone has something
they must do today, even if it is another form of waiting
or a leading of each other through the hours that are left.

.

There it is still. That same longing to step above love
and see eternity. But beyond that last
breakthrough lie such cold dead spaces, full of everything
and nothing that stays. What need is there for voids,
endlessly available as they've become? What can we bring
back from them? Or else at least, before you leave,
run your hands over the stones in the backyard and see just how
much the ground belongs to you. Which is to say, our constantly
shifting size. Constant love of air and soil. Regardless of
the structures we've arranged our spaces in, there will be
that one spot in which the maps and numbers
we've collected vanish.

Only the light that hits our eyes as we exit the building.
Only words sung by new genders in the simple dawn.
Only cables coiled on a table, steps accompanied
by the sounds of empty towns, crushed paper, lost cars
gleaned through fog. Only messages deciphered
in our absence. Only echoes of engines that failed in the wind
after setting the pace of our lives. Only endless replacements,
the music that pushed us into love despite everything. Only
transit. Only every dull reversal of the world. Only a song's
shape guiding the movements of a dredged-up heart.

·

She throws her gaze into the leaves, and it dangles there.
The light and the dark and the hours they float in pass by.
She keeps pieces of pedestrian conversations safe on shelves.
Each winter we sit in the living room and share the news.
In our dreams, perfected things fall back to what is ancient
and are lost to us. We're supposed to keep looking for new ways
of connecting the dots. I just want to be left alone sometimes.
That fear of adults being something other than what we're
capable of understanding. So what are we now? All these
light bulbs sinking in the sea. I've been seeing strangers with
familiar faces talking of how time tore up and scattered them
again.

·

How many years has it been since your last flu shot?
The day took a strange direction as he waited for his hour
to pass. Like amnesiacs running into mirrors, the revelation
of ourselves fills us with the heaviness of impossible wants.
Somehow we came out of all the non-retractable
decisions of the water and the slowly dancing continents we walk.
I just wanted to say hello. I remember, for instance,
how to drive a car. The feeling of being reduced to a limited
operator of gears, a speeding up of the town. The give-
and-take of human measures. Finding strangers sitting
beside us in waiting rooms with good views of ticking clocks.

A house full of sweat and heat pipes, showers and toilets
and windows and flowers arranged in glass vases. Crumbs
like tiny boulders dotting the blue-tiled countertops and wooden
island. Sunlight filling bedrooms in the morning where the
grown children sleep. Waking, then the small routines. Stains on
couches and sheets that no one has noticed. Standing over
sinks filling the first glass of the day. Looking out the window
at the neighbor's kitchen, the edge of a fridge just visible.
Going over checklists in our heads as we step out
into the spaces we do not control. For a moment forgetting
what emergencies feel like.

.

That little ghost in natural colors. The part of
a loved one's memory that animates all objects around it.
The wet grime on the walls on the day that it rained. There
was a movie on, about tea houses in the time just before
the New Year's when we boarded the subway at midnight
and the cars were empty, the sound of fireworks above us
inaudible. Pictures falling on a hardwood floor echo
into daydreams at the tail-end of the ten percent
that we remember. The sirens still calling from their stony
mounds, telling you they know you, that they saw you once
in a crowded hall, a bit nervous, as if waiting for the world's
haggard spirits to arrive by tank.

.

I know that if it rains, I will look for an umbrella. Or I'll
wait inside, flipping through pages, making coffee, or sitting
on the stairs scrolling through names. By any measure
we've sustained the damage we could. And still later
we'll spend the days walking around buildings,
waiting for more. I've been meaning to go back and record
over the errors, but this city in the lit-up fog has kept me
from minding time. The disease that killed a friend's father
is making headlines. For now, we get to look at diagrams
of what things could be. Claiming our separate rights
to watch, to judge the unfurling of our small decisions.
Letting the dishes sit for a week.

Every night, he wraps himself in the voices of the people who
taught him to sing. The attempts keep him warm. Waiting for each
second to pass becomes a job of isolating one by one the
parts of him. The winter long ago when he returned, almost grown,
to the town that birthed him is still wedged
in his ribs. That winter, he found he no longer knew the slang
and lacked the effortless manner in which his relatives
who stayed delivered it. The small bed where he now sleeps
sits next to a framed view of neighboring rooftops.
Nothing more alone than a clear mind.

.

The pilgrim woke at the bottom of a brand new sea
and looking at his hands, knew he'd become a small
digital ghost. And he called up to his body, which was floating
face up on the surface, its pupils entranced by the skies.
In the cities the bombs had fallen with the majesty
of gods shitting. In bedrooms citizens drank
and listened to reports, speaking the necessary words
of kindness. Pedestrians dreamt under layers of smoke
and fluorescent lighting. The country's unhinged minds
drifted down the streets, to the sea.

As ready and able as conscious ghosts, we let go. The ground
opens to let our old bones inside. Strangers' gazes rest
on us from time to time, and then move on.
The willows in the park with the artificial lake sway like
days in a life of houses
        made to fade. The mind opposing the
desperate kind of dance and the mind dreaming in its patterns.
The young man in his room dividing himself into canvases
and the young man waking up to find drooping branches
moving over him. Plain daylight shines on the covers, the air
in the room showing its dust.

.

Sometimes I step outside amazed that we still
get up to do this each day. Even this doom
of a god that remains absent is a way world opens.
We walk to the town with our stacks of papers
and instruments slung over our backs. Some of us
carry sins in the small pouches stitched to the insides
of our jackets, there for the day when they will
come in handy. We practice juggling lives ten at a time.
If only we had infinity and a few more arms to point
to the receding answers. For now we make do
with tracing our bruises, as if they were lights
that could bring us home.

.

She never wanted to disappear into usefulness.
She wanted the effortless earth to throw her off, wanted
to climb to the rooftop to nap on the artificial grass.
She wanted a place that flaws could enter
unconcealed. She got up in front of her lover each morning
and changed. In the confusion of speakers, she wanted to hear
the actual bell tolls making the insides of our monuments hum.
She wanted to store and burn what the days left over.
She wanted each sound to be the last of its kind.

The urns and the manuscripts in the museum went
quickly. This was the state of the distant turmoil
broadcast to us. Old men who've lived and will die at the foot
of mountains, believing the rigidity of their days proved
they still knew something. Old men of tomorrow, under awnings
exhaling smoke into the rain. That the key to the balcony above
the yard still works makes him pause. He enters the fresh
air, the unfiltered elements drifting in the evening,
and he breathes as they erode him away. If he dies here,
he imagines, the breeze will take his smell. If he dies here,
the train will pass below on rusted tracks that dangle
above freeways, between stacks of tenements.

.

In the dream nobody aged. All the years returned. Every
object revealed the need that pulled it from the earth.
Each time our hands held them, the leaves writhed in their
crystalline structures. Raindrops took days to float down.
We met on sidewalks and saw in each other's eyes
what the morning had carved. Words were hardly necessary.
We wandered entranced by the unfamiliar buildings asleep
on their sides. The wide gazes of animals opened us.
Over glass shards we made our way to the end of a valley.
I found the house I'd always wanted, in the mountains. I found
the only screen available for miles filing the hours away.

.

No more standing in a circle. No more birds of paradise.
No steel frames. No rules nailed to doors. No more doors.
No more waiting for the right grip to raise the wrench.
No dogs. No cats. No dragonflies. No elk. No sleepless
sharks floating quiet in dark waters. No more golden
feminine laughter. No elders. No clear skies. No wasted
hunger. No more cleansing rain. No flowerbeds. No rails
No stems. No proper names. No safety words. No walls.
No more childhood ponds. No dining by the shore. No
more wine. No more music left in the caves we tagged.
No bread. No roads. No working castles. No close
listeners of echoes. No more comfortable songs.

There seemed to be no words that could express this need.
We simulated distress with pupils spread to the size of islands, like
dogs biting their way out of a myth to offer their throats before being
drowned out by the sound of aircraft pulsing through layers of fog.
Yet none of it clicks. All the little nerve endings of human
choices fissure just out of reach. The viewer can't tell
her exact location on the road to the destitute times. There's no
grasping that moment when things break and a new world
is born from what we've lost. Or rather I was hoping
that there really were no endings. Just the places
where we stop naming our parts

.

Today is all blue with no clouds. A third of the moon
hangs in the eastern sky. In the brightly lit lunch room,
afterhours, I listen to the footsteps of co-workers
in the office next door. The end of the year again. People
talking of potential resolutions. Me with time running out,
playing with the lighter in my pocket. Counting this
moment and the one after that one and this one now.
Waiting in my chair and muttering under my breath.
I could sleep through this, be alive in some other way.

.

Hallway steps   pages
    the bottom of   swallowing words
known to cause   goodbyes
    on cardstock   floating over blacked out
screens   taking the path laid out   discovered
  in stages   the sky   from the outside
    mimicking the war   death patterns arranged
to go viral   types of tragedies familiar   those who wait
   can see the unedited   plumes of metal
    unclasped   fell to the bed   with the rest
of her skin   the naked eye   blinking out

The mountains where he and his horse would sometimes
wait out the rain under the shelter of rock overhangs
still sit under the sky, far away, without agendas. Their air alive
with wet branches. Caves opening their jaws to the low
mists of spring. Water running into town. Trucks
full of sugar cane rattling down curving roads, the radios throwing music
and sales pitches into the trees. Rusted machetes, abandoned roadside
or left hidden in tall grass. In the hospital, he dreams the same places
over and over. The hand of the nurse is slow and soft
as it raises the metal spoon to his lips. The needles stay cold
in the veins of his arms. Thick plastic curtains separate the beds.
The kids are sometimes brought to look at him and the bright
green numbers on the monitors changing.

.

As it were. As the wires we've set up
begin to tangle. As everything gets spoken out of time.
As we drive all night in solitary lanes. As it stands.
As the struggle to stay drunk continues to the sound
of small fractures. As whole buildings dedicated to particular
bones collapse into decades of sprawl. As junkies read
by starlight the symbols embossed on their skin.
As rain rattles the lake and the rooftops of the future
where the newborns who survived us gaze out
at the lights.

.

You always run the risk of losing friends, but that's not
what matters here. A blackbird dents the air as it swivels mid-
flight and darts into an alley. It's without your lover
that you see your age again. The work and blunders
you've put in. From this point on, each step is final, each
step has a thousand future ghosts inside. Smile like you
mean it, but keep your eyes glued to the outlines. Play your
guitar with crushed nails and watch the blackbird swatches
slash the air above the workday. Don't expect any rewards.

The statue of the man stands in the public park in a circle
of evergreens. The inscription states the obvious: feeling obliged
to put up hopeless resistance, he was cast in bronze. Of his enemies,
the ones who still live like to spend some mornings sitting on the
nearby benches, staring at the features the sculptor rendered.
I pass by and head toward the man-made pond. While watching
the water, it hits me that my father's getting older and more pensive.
I try to picture him walking alone as a young man down some street
on the coast. Confused and surprised that work came to him
in time. Wondering if love would grow to overflow him. Missing
the sounds of his first language. Suspecting certain joys
would never happen again.

.

Spring would catch us. It would see us trying so hard
to cry like animals and would surround us with curious
plants that could feed on our leftovers when the time came.
In the clearing provided, we could kneel and disgorge ourselves
over and over, and out of our entrails would come the smell
of our neighbors, the stench of blood, and processed meals
and bits of dream. If we could learn to cry like that, each time
we flung the door of a new house open, perhaps
we could remember all the things gone, in precise detail,
without trying. It might surprise us how much the moment
we both stood in our boats looking up at the bridges at night
could unhinge us.

.

Time to see again. Waking in his old bed: an awful feeling.
He puts on his shoes, pants, a warm jacket and a cashmere cap,
and he walks west along the highway, passing walled shopping
centers, the sky massive, the cars speeding past him three
feet away. He gets to the ocean and walks north along the road
that curves up the coast. There's no plan, except to walk.
This, he thinks, is how I'll spend my youth. By late evening
he has made it to the harbor at the northern edge of town.
His feet pulse with a dull pain. He sits on a bench and listens
to the sailboats tap against the docks.

If the instructions say to leave the comfort of whatever
we call home to rebuild our language piece by piece
in streets that don't know us, let me grab my coat.
I've packed a lunch. We can eat it outside, by the river,
and watch the vapor of our social dreams receding
from the skyline. In this place that's spinning
round the sun, I have walked to your door and called
your name. I've held you on the ledges of tall buildings
and searched for your hair in crowds of insane actors
playing with fire under blinking satellites and singing
of how strange it is to be.

.

He picks up a leaf from the sidewalk. This seems childish.
Right where he wants to be but can't. Neurotic small
chameleon looking for music. Anticipating all the while
the need for falling limply so as not to break. Holding out
in fallout shelters, writing waltzes on bare thighs with markers,
trying not to count days. Sanity requires withholding certain
information from yourself, or else being okay with breaking
what your hands have held so far. He quickly gives
the leaf back to the sidewalk. The traffic comes back
into focus. The book he holds says a thing of beauty
is annoyed forever. Be prepared to start over every few days.

.

I toss and turn for hours. The dream of perfection
leaves me as the dream of good old honest failure
crosses my mind. The possible bursts of flight that might
come of it. Though on most days our minds don't convene.
We keep colliding in the hope that one day the word
will match the image, but we have no pure channels
through which to fall and land at the weightless center
of each other's slow dying. We can sense it barely,
stuck in our hands. And we say that it's enough
to just be close. To see you across from me,
doing all the things worth doing badly.

Let the earthquakes have their way. Let your skin
flake off without anger. Let your particles follow
their paths of decay and feel yourself in them
settling on the room's surfaces. Let the hesitation
in your lover's speech stand for the distance he must travel
to your bed. Let sleeping ghosts wake. Let the cold light
wash over your house. Let the walls of the world go to war.
Let the rocket's glare light your way to the water
where the pier stands firm against the fog. Let the children
with their sweat-drenched bodies mosh
in tender violence as the years fall off and burst
upon the planks.

.

The train crosses the length of the rearview mirror
like a massive animal gone in a blue metal blur. The tracks
run through the middle of the shopping district,
which shines today with sunlight and manicured trees.
The worms that make their temporary homes
in the forking branches are rolling over in their sleep,
falling from leaf to leaf like water drops. People
are forgetting already that it rained. The letters
they sent are descending over distant cities. Cup your
hands and remember, you don't need a shell.

.

After the first years of youth we found the beach
almost without sand. We smoked and watched
birds taking off and landing on wet rocks. Swirls of smoke
escaped our mouths into the cold and became
lines of gray that faded. The next day
and the ones after it arrived sooner than we could adjust
to the new kinds of lighting invented in the intervening hours.
In the street, you limped from a broken toe
and said you felt old. My friend, I still remember the camp
where we first met. I too strain each day to gather
my scattered chances.

A feeling survived   is what we have
          So don't look forward
      and toss the stage   and not backwards
        Not angels not humans
                    On the grass
Alternating currents of sound from the windy city
   Cry of the train in the gridworks of light and steel
scaffoldings   We feed our tickets to small
stout machines   Not from the sky but from
          the center of the lungs   Our lives
subtracted   make way

                    •

Ants can fall forever and be fine. But you,
favored prodigies of the small digital evening,
running in the cold, down escalators, into trains, speeding
underground on filthy cushions, wild and overgrown,
are utterly transformed by the smallest stumbling. I was ordering
a drink when you called. I hear they're learning to collide
particles at such high speeds that we might all accidentally
be teleported to a stranger's bathroom, naked and alone,
staring out the window at thin branches swaying in a metal town.
We'll shiver from the spasm of displacement
and steel ourselves to open the door.

                    •

The girl with flushed cheeks in the morning rises
from bed, drowsy. How she can seem so unaware of her
effect on me (animals falling from the sky with no explanations)
I'll never know. Like forgetting how lips open.
Everything feels weary this millennium. But today,
today will be different. We're going to bash our faces
against glass. Replay the violence in slow motion. This
self-witnessing is hypnotic in its simplicity, works
as a nightlight for hours. But you woke me. You were
dancing in your underwear. Singing in a voice so sweet
my days aged inside it.

We're dying to give ourselves away, but fumble.
The flicker of customized ads is distracting.
We slowed down as we approached the end of arguments,
afraid there would be nothing afterward, that our past
declarations would prove larger than us. The small cry
of one man to another, we get to hold none of its weight,
just the snapshots of all the places it compelled us to see.
All those stars with price tags that we stole, the walkways
the radio left in my sleep.

.

Like glass vases dropped from rooftops. Our
continents spread in fractals on the floor. I built this one
from the sounds of all the underpasses that we
walked through in our younger days, holding up our
cellphone screens to light the way, speaking in hushed
voices so as not to wake the vagabonds. This one
we made from the accelerated years that memories
rendered vast and porous. From every sky, the music that we
saved, rain collected in plastic buckets, falls on our heads.
From branches, spiders sense the wind as it plays
with our dust.

.

The hills are swiveling. And we're hardly able to describe
our own horizons. We buy each other lunch and spit out
reverberating waves of sound to say
        I can feel the bones in my hands, and soon
I'll be a tree. But first we'll lie under the planes, the waves,
the rooftops of the cities that we left and still carry
like impractical hearts. Hearing every day
the ragged air we inherited and must now stray
and sing and die inside of. With each swivel, a pale shiver
drives our search for some new patch of inhuman space.

Every day, notes remembered, notes lost. I make the small
adjustments in my head. My friends' eyes are always changing,
the distance that can't be helped becoming apparent.
And that we both see it means we try to speak not louder
but in a pitch that might maneuver through the barriers
of perspective and get us across to the clearing where we're trying
with numb hands to build a fire. Out in the streets
we're flanked by signals and identical expressions of a life
in common. Near the entrance to a store of lost records,
I pull out my phone and search for a familiar name.

.

Who are these desperate gathered? According to sources
village elders are leaving their mountains to see the lights
of the city where cameras are capturing the flashes of heat
and displaced flesh as they happen. All I can give you
are my eyes. Here are the parks so green, the air
of the supermarkets so pleasant. The streets are rigid
and clean. Our buildings loom over us. Lights
on the patio of the old hotel, children placing their hands
around artificial fires. Survival measures include talking.
Sharing a box of take-out. Waiting. Knowing when to ask
a friend a question if they're lost in thought.

.

The edge of our losses, when not immeasurable,
is shaped like the outline of our favorite faces. They once
were soft and turning slowly in the afternoon.
A narrow path between the trees leads to a ledge
where we sat once and watched people below
weaving their lives into the buildings and the streets.
Later, driving north across the plains, we tossed
unwritten pages out the window. Stopped in fields for
bread water and fruit, the day surrounding us with all
its elements in high relief. We splayed on the grass
and spent the afternoon letting our fingers
calcify.

Your children are pulling guns on everyone because they
have to. Your children are watching the line behind them
getting longer than the line ahead. They're exiting their cars
while overhead, sirens cry in the cold air that reveals nothing
and is endless. Your children hold on to each other's eyes
as they go on their own inward ways. Your children leave their
skins in each other's eyes. They book their lives ahead of waking
and get broken and repaired over and over. Your children get
gray-haired and forgetful and do not grow up. Your children
can be found under the rocket's light, making love to fight music,
giving each other a thousand new names and taking them off again
gently, like earrings.

.

We turned at last to the image of our own derailed train.
It was falling from the bridge into the river.
In cushioned chairs the sleepers dreamt their little bright
eternities. The waking saw their lives rising to meet them.
But today we are still in our beds, waiting half-conscious
for alarm clocks to sound. Then wide-eyed, in awe
of our own hands that keep wrinkling. The room
imprinting its colors in the morning. Empty bottles
on the windowsill refract sunlight a dark gold.
A day the color of parking lots and transplanted trees
waits for us to put on clothes.

Then the girl is a woman holding the old heartbreaks
in her hand. She walks from the station, steps blending
into the city's cacophony. Miles to the east, the fields
are orange with sunset. She has accepted
all her future endings. She can call up any friend
and let the minutes pass, filing her realizations in silence
as crowds go in and out of the district's glass doors.
From a bench, she watches snow falling on the bay
for the first time in decades.

.

In winter, regrets become icicles that drop in our sleep.
Some mornings we put off choosing our outfits
for as long as possible. Light cigarettes on patios
and talk about the weather. Walk to corner stores
with hands stuffed in our pockets, the drone
of working heaters in the evenings seeing us to sleep.
A lover is this shape of cured glass, brimming with
unknowns and surfaces. I place each thought of you
inside a fold of my window's yellow curtains and
lie there, not sleeping, putting off the morning
awhile longer.

.

When the world came to the village, the villagers
stood like children in the flood of new objects.
The unfamiliar metals and floating lights filled
the night with phosphorescence. And the village
slowly ceased. The young sons, who once had been
boys running in the muddy streets, were now thousands
of miles away, living in the small rooms of a dreamed
empire, ordering take-out, glowing in the screenlight,
letting time slip and their vocabularies loosen.
They stopped asking themselves long ago,
What names did I forget today?

Helping one select, for an adjustable fee, how to be free in a cage
We grew up and arrived at the supermarkets and bars
To realize that nothing there wanted change and
Bought a postcard for a friend, wrote a toast
We wanted all sorts of change. Walked out, crossed the street
For the moments that we used and are now gone, everywhere
And forever. I wanted to say, on the walk home
I nodded good luck to some pigeons—to say
As we smoked on the patio, the sky black and full

.

But that was another room, that August. I remember
the bare wood of the bed frame. The soft covers
on our faces. Your hair on the pillow's white fabric.
Falling asleep at two in the morning. Seas clutching our
brains and pulling us down. We remember only
flashes later while sitting in the backseat of a car
watching the steel cranes of the docks outlined against the
orange bay. The light-rail glides by, its windows
replying to the sun, the airport's glass rooftop blinding.
As we approach the bridge, I can feel last hour's choices
hardening steadily into all I have.

.

The white ceramic cup sits atop the granite
table. The windows of the shop are open
and a breeze weaves itself into the summer heat
that's been collecting in the room since morning. Like
reptiles in the sun, the middle-aged women by the pool
dreamlessly sleep. Or I fancy them dreamless. It hasn't
rained in a while and won't for many months. I imagine
this same place five years from now. A sadder and more
tired me, groping around for another good reason
to sit at my table and work.

At night, from the hill, the freeways looked like streams
of disembodied lights. We thought in silence
about our own particular endings. Three of us
sitting on the stone bench, drinking. Below, the town
with its scattered sounds. Bark of a dog in someone's yard.
A nearby birdcall. Occasional boom of artillery tests
from the military base just north. My friend played
his guitar with cold hands, placing his half-smoked cigarette
between two strings by the tuning knobs. Practical habit
glowing orange in the dark.

·

The girl stood closer to him so as to force
his attention. To leave no space in his field of vision
for doubt to seep in. Winds carrying particles
of radiation washed over town. Stray gusts brushed
her face, moving strands of hair that had been resting
on her cheeks and over her eyes. This millennium
we begin again the long fragmenting dream.
I know nothing, he said, I look out from this shape
and touch you clumsily with as much of my scattered
mind as possible. Yes, she said, this shape.
These fingers on my skin.

·

The gods did nothing but invite us to believe our senses.
Then, almost by accident, we stumbled one day
into the nothingness where these same gods
built their beds and spend occasional eternities looking
down at our childish days. Our ways have gone on
for so long that we can't remember them not being.
And these glimpses we stumble upon quickly fade,
till we forget what it was that caused our fear. We look up
from our books in apartments and houses where the walls
collect our smells, the notes in our voices, our stares.

We were stuck in a canvas of splattered days. Restrained
flumes of feeling breaking against buildings, digesting
ourselves, growing insane from ourselves. I wanted to stand
like the sea cliffs. I wanted to step outside of my mind's
door and be under an open sky, be where the unrestrained
sits still. In the lit hallways of familiar houses our steps
echo. I take hold of the edge of the old desk in the
dusty light of a summer and breathe. Burning these
flowers day in and day out is beginning to drain me.
All this ash: where to hide it? Through closed eyes
I see you arguing in an empty field.

.

As if it were your first dead animal. As if
we were made of glass and had been tossed in the air
for a lifetime. As if we could forget entirely
that we'll eventually reflect light in dull waves.
As if part of us could stay in the spaces we leave.
As if time weren't coiled inside you. As if our hearts
could find some larger form to contain them. As if
we could unlace from our bodies. As if our objects
could forget us and become their own music-box world.

.

Everything comes back, whether or not you've managed
to change in the intervening hours. Our non-choices too
fling us ahead. Today in our screens: live shots
of resistance under fire. A brief scene from our trip
to the island in October. Spines cracking as backs
stretch in the morning. If only we could be
as prepared for the day as we are once the day's
been through with us. Naked toes against
hardwood floors. Voicemails waiting
in the wires.

When it cleared, we found ourselves standing
with our feet in the tide pools, the tide low,
our hands empty. Saying thank you as the meanings
of our words died on our lips and fell to the water
like stones. The sun rose and draped the cove gold.
An exploded core spilling its bright melt
on the slivers of the ocean's face.
We stood there, shin-deep in water. The salt
marking our wounds. Our hands saying thank you
as hermit crabs walked by our feet.

.

What's needed is an attitude of nonresistance
to the world. A good grip along the edges of it.
A way to hold yourself along while the breakneck
spillage of its nations washes over you. Let the
wreckage of its wars pass untouched. Make way
for all our failures. Just this: to sit, like lizards.
To lie, even, like lizards, under the battered atmosphere,
basking in the light of all phenomena, not moving
at all as bullets rain down, being happy at the sight
of another's eyes, watching together the violent
landings, the flower-like bursts of dirt clouds.

.

A people's movement, says the woman
in the suit, holding her script above her head
like it might protect her. The people, she says,
are moving and their voices are being replaced
by displays of despair. The glass sides
of the buildings mirror the crowds. Over them
hang thin clouds shaped like sand dunes.
Through the tear gas they caught a couple
kissing by the cement barricades.

A country of masks. A country where rain
can be danced into lifting.
                A country remembered
as empty streets where you played as children.
A country that slaughters precisely, clean of hands.
A country of self-spectators and glass harbors.
A country playing to the logical end its dream
of selfhood. A country awake in a day of traffic,
faint moon hanging in the clear afternoon.

                        .

The sound of ducks in the artificial lake across
the freeway sneaks into my dream, where a firefly
has landed on my face and melted through. Dissonance
wakes me. The bed feels like an open hand and I stare out
from something weightless. Something whispers:
The signs you're waiting for are there, overlooked,
ahead, or inside you, unwritten. Get up. There is
no one in the kitchen. There's coffee to make.
It takes a few minutes to adjust to the sunlight.

                        .

When we were done with childhood, we drank
and smoked and agreed that a defeated generation could not
be mourned. On the balcony, laughing and flushed
for a moment with belief. The old balm about how
everything that disappears is returning somewhere
almost felt tangible, as if there, just on the other side
was being alive. We strapped ourselves to the minutes,
trying not to be afraid. I've said "See you around"
many times, but knew each time that I might not.

Blind insects fly in the dark and occasionally
bump against the pilgrim's face. The path winds
under the freeway and goes past the last rows
of identical houses at the edge of the city. He never
knows what to say when people ask him where
he's going. There's no point in walking but to walk.
Each morning is a process of remembering his hands,
the legs and feet that carry him, the nights turned
to silver tatters in his pockets.

.

The veins under the marble resemble lines of sea foam.
The coffee in my veins helps keep my hands in constant
motion. I have one cigarette left, behind my ear.
The miles of rail that would connect us, dear friend,
this afternoon lie gleaming in the valleys, gathering
heat in perfect solitude. I can pluck no answers
from the humid afternoon. Love is draining, and yet
I wish you more of it. That it might fill you past
completion, give you music as you step into a crowd,
make you borderless

.

When the bridges folded, we sought solace in the words
of our past minds, found ways to praise ourselves,
aware we were nonetheless falling apart.
Here the only option is to start
forgetting everything. On the rooftops of the city,
we look up and write the stars down in our tablets,
renaming each of them at whim. Only impulse
can save us. A jolt of need. We trade goodbyes
like digital animals in dying clothes.

During the blackout, I sat at my desk
The candles shifted their gentle yellow glow
A glass of wine, stacks of paper, a cell phone
Spliced with a sudden doubt, as if now
Like messages moving underwater, forever bent
To an old phrase my mother used to say
To reflect light, as it enters the eye and
The futures we abandon with every choice made
On the inside of our skulls, their primal shapes

                    .

As I fell, I closed my eyes and imagined flying.
The pain of landing was almost absurd in its
unexpectedness. But it was final.
Every night I am forced to face my boundaries. Every
day a search for a breaking point that proves elusive.
In our boredom we meet, strangers feeling kinship,
as if we sense for the first time a connection
that we used to possess, and whose loss we,
distanced by consciousness and flesh, have no way
to shake off.

                    .

Of the two, it's pain that has the keener edge.
This chipping away of one's connections keeps us
watching: tendons sliced open, leaving behind
two lonely pieces of skin. This is us
in our beds, dreaming of separate caves. In a building
of collapsing stairs, I contemplated pleasure.
The body of a stranger beside me. From inside
her sleep, a voice was saying, There are tigers in the hallways.
Our cages melted. We had no idea where to go.

On the screen were the pictures of our long ago
walk on the pier. Your hair before the water.
In the headlines we tossed in the fire, we thought
we could make out familiar names.
The ruins of the jetty. The skyline
across the bay. In one picture your hair
frames your mouth, which is parted, perhaps
in the middle of sounding a word. There was
a loveliness to the way you spilled your wine.
I wasted so much time looking for napkins.

.

Next to the generator, a patch of tall weeds
sways with breeze. The steel poles from which the
traffic lights hang bob up and down lightly. The white
freeway walls are peeling. On concrete benches
people wait, for evening, for rain, for calls.
A hummingbird floats above an empty lot. From a
hard plastic bus seat, a woman looks out at the asphalt
blurring by. Everything is going somewhere.
The power plant's gray fumes blend into the low, gray
clouds. The tide is way out. Blind to its own end
the hummingbird moves in eternity.

.

Strangely, our joy is to feel like giants, to float
down avenues on massive wings. But we all
open our eyes eventually, even if it's simply
to check the clock, to breathe and see
how we remain in our frames. We stand in front
of paintings and try to see them from the inside.
Our eyes curve around the paint, which was laid
on the canvas, between smoke breaks, by some
painter who thought he felt everything, ages ago.

Do you recall that spring? We paused to hear the sound
of the waves. The crashes carried in the wind that
shook the branches under which we napped.
In the afternoon we woke, and fumbled off our clothes.
Forgot our names and said nothing for hours.
These islands of youngness keep my mind company.
Do you remember the organ playing its song
in the living room in winter? Everyone was high
and sharing cigarettes on the back porch. I carry
these days in my cells, cells that keep dividing
and dying off.

.

He made us from flesh after much self-debate
and obsession. He made mountains filled
with the metals we needed to transcend the sky.
He made weeping trees and insects that burst
from the rivers. He made frogs and ravines
and ghosts to live in the caves. He made hunters
and prey and men who would die for intangible things.
And once it was finished, he turned himself
into a small brown cricket, and set himself down
on a patch of grass, to live and die in his creation,
having made himself forget he ever made anything.

.

Skyscraper creatures of stillness. Metal structures
summoned from our oldest fears. Saved sounds
flooding headphones. Chopin's fingers
run their breath over the faces of the five-
o'clock crowd. On the avenue, the wide eyes
of a curious toddler pass by and leave
their kernel in my evening. The wait
at the station, the sound of the subway train
rushing toward us, competing gusts of wind
filling the underground atrium, the airbrushed
bodies in the ads on the concrete walls.

When it gets dark, the trees come down and
whisper in the old man's ear all kinds of things.
That the seas are overflowing. That the sugar cubes
in the kitchen are crumbling. That this will be
his coldest winter yet. That his lucky animal today
is the blind cat. That there are sirens by the harbor
and he should not waste time. That a storm is coming
to wash his house clean of photographs. He listens
only half-awake, wondering where the trees find all
those voices. If it's the wind that wakes them up.

.

Since life has come down to a series of "I want"
statements, my friend said into the phone, I want
just for the swallowing of days to be less painful.
I want to own a ship, I said, and to spend my time in
peace watching the coastlines shrink.
Do you want food? he asked. Do you want the
company of the women you've known? Do you want
God to appear from the air and help you pass
the hours with invented stories of how things began?
No. Just good vision and a simple stare. And when I finally
hit land, I want to stay in the way the sand glows
during red tide when my feet step on it.

.

Beyond all borders
lie more borders, so why is it that we sometimes want
to drift forever? Lure of transgression? The need
to be known? There is a place where none of that
matters, a place where all of us stands bare and
part of everything. A place where we are not, and
words match their melodies. Here in this room
overlooking a road on which ambulances from
the nearby hospital pass each day, the books
on my shelf stolidly bear my days' dust, and even in
the wailing of the sirens there's a silence to be found.

Suddenly the lovers are at sea, shark-infested
waters of pure happiness. Had you forgotten all
about this? No, but

    When I wake up, I'm in the belly of a
dull machine, all my longings are for sale and
I have no money to buy them back

    We were in the backseat of a car, coming
to terms. The clouds had unified and the whole
sky was gray and we kissed for rain

        Delirious, bit each other's tongues and
jumped into the salty water

·

We've done, over the years, the worst already.
The question is now how to live afterwards.
The answer is too simple for us. Which is to say,
under your seat you will find not a single flotation device.
Have an ice cream cone. I'm serious. Sit on a park bench
some morning and don't try to forget how the human
world is falling to insanity. Just hold the knowledge
inside you as you watch the crowds. Everything is
as your elders taught you. There were never safety nets.
Nothing to blind you from your place.

·

A short walk from my grandmother's farm
there was a waterfall. I remember my mother could
dive from the top of it into the pool below and
somehow survive, intact and smiling, every time.
From the pool itself, I watched amazed, my arms
wrapped around the inner tube of a large tractor
tire, my only guarantee of buoyancy. Though I feared
drowning, I loved the feeling of my body being held
in water, my feet dangling in that strange,
not–human realm.

They watched the approaching masses, side by side
Under the sky, which was supposed to belong
As the lights at the crosswalk changed and all was motion
Everyone. Together. At the count of three
I woke up because I thought I recognized your shoulders
In the crowd, and I didn't want to dream of
That morning the air tasted of recent rain
She looked in the mirror as she put on her earrings, and asked
Her just-woken voice brushing aside the last grains of my sleep
Have we been ourselves lately? Today?

·

     Before it's over you're allowed
to freak out endlessly. I never had control
to begin with, over the patterns of the day or the
movement of bodies. I can only move, as whole as
possible, through my scheduled shifts, the minutes spent
at intersections, the hours browsing shelves,
the evenings at my desk, waiting for sleep. Wandering
through parking structures, stepping out into a night
filled with couples walking, in thick jackets, to the theater,
friends gathered to relearn the art of falling
on any kind of ground.

·

The spotted shade of the tree branches moves
over the surface of my shoes and over the surface of
the sidewalk, which is old and stained with the dried
juices of ripe berries that have fallen and been squished.
When I see some high school kid at the station trying
to flirt with a girl, getting self-conscious, and the girl,
sure of her beauty, getting bored and waiting for
him to say something that will at least let her laugh,
I think *this must be paradise*. This weightless
fleeting hour where a man asks me for a quarter,
and I have to say *sorry*, and he walks away.

My advice to her was always impractical. Never rush
wakefulness. Pray for me to whatever you believe in
when you throw off the sheets. Keep an eye out
for the dreams of man that are toppling like sugar statues.
Know that things seem simpler in moonlight.
Every word is someone's fate, and you can sing
all of them. Today I stepped into the skin of my feet
and paced around the house for an hour.
There are clearings in the forest only the lost
can find.

The earth has no particular hurry. It answers
our migrations with the occasional earthquake,
with birdsong to astonish our steelwork, the perpetual
collapsing of the waves. Out on the patio, the lights turn on
after we've been under the sensors a few seconds.
Tonight the wind spins above us and sometimes hits
an audible pitch. My materials include a room, a laptop,
pen, paper, and some pocket change. I waited by a foggy
road today, anxious for home. I'd been told
not to let everything depend on a twist of grace,
which might fall on the wrong person, or not at all.

Tourists walk the trails, passing by bushes of dead
dry flowers and splayed skeletal leaves. A mist
floats through the pines. Groups looking to be awed
pause at the benches to take pictures. They jump or
make faces and otherwise struggle to create a moment
they'll want to remember. There's as yet no way to capture
the effect of a gust of wind on one's contemplation
of dry plants. The rattlesnakes stay hidden in the rocks.
At the lookout point, after the tourists leave, it's just
me and a bee hovering by the signpost staked
at the edge of the cliff.

How do we live with surveillance footage of a dying
child being ignored by passersby in an outdoor
market? The answer is, of course, the same way
we've lived with it before. That day, I closed
the browser, collected my things, and walked to work.
Arrived early and found no one there. Read a few pages
from a book, distractedly, then stared at the new
art on the walls. The pleasantness of the colors
bothered me. At night I stood by my bed and wondered
where I'd put my phone, knowing tomorrow I'd wake
into a world that had gone on changing as I slept.

Our escapes from ordinary life were planned in delirium,
and now, with the alarm clock ringing, our shirts half on
and our hair in a tangle, we are faced with the problem
of execution. How good that it's cloudy and the sky
seems a thick ceiling of mist. In the saturated
freeway lanes, we sip our coffees and listen
to the news. We tunnel through the noise for hours
while the sight of passing trees reminds us of a distant urge.
What if you stepped out of the car during the traffic jam
and walked around greeting your neighbors?

Cigarette ash swirls in the puddle the rain left
on the table. From the veranda on the
third floor, I have a view of the back parking lot
and the rooftop of a nearby, shorter building.
There's no one else in sight, no recording equipment
to witness me. I make no signals of any kind.
The deeper color of things after rain almost promises
warmth. Shiny metal generators litter the rooftop.
All's quiet on the asphalt with its painted lines.
In the distance the red lights of a power plant
seem to think in time.

They are so young. Skinny jeans and winter jackets.
A lovely vanity moves their faces. These, it hits me,
are the same kids I saw on the bus earlier today. Now
with night upon everyone, they look a bit tired.
They lean their heads on each other's shoulders,
their silence a comfortable one. Secure in their beauty,
they keep the world at bay. In a few minutes they'll be
jaywalking across the boulevard, laughing, silhouetted
in headlights.

The pilgrim sees himself ahead, ending in his own hands
like a failed plant. He traces the outline of his face and it
almost calms him to think that nothing very large
could possibly reside in such narrowness. Between the blades
of grass, the bees dance their language. Jet planes streak
silently the pale dome of the sky. An empty slab of road stretches
all the way to the horizon. Distant gas station lamppost
flickers to life. He puts his palms on the ground
and feels the ache in his legs draining. Holds on like a rabbit
waiting for a hawk's shadow to pass.

For life is a briefness
we carry calmly on an average day. That's how it works,
said the old man. You get to be young for a long time
then you start getting old. Days grow full of reminders
of past lives. Objects and words start containing
so much more than their initial definitions, and it becomes
almost laughable to try to speak them. This is why
we learn each other's language every time. To speak
despite the fact that, say, you are blind
and I am sleeping.

After all our violent failures to meet, the one thing
we can fully share is this distance. Where you've
arrived and where I am look over the same
span of cities. In movable shelters, I sit after work
and think of how lives tangle and confuse
themselves in each other. A lover's agreement reads:
When you gain I will gain, when you lose I will
lose, and in the hour of your death I will be halved.
But when love ends and we are both alive, what then?
When the tangled parts are displaced? When odd
fractions of us break away and we're left standing?

The transfixed man dropped his pen
and grew deaf to the sounds of rush hour.
Metal trees catch our covert signals. This slow
passing workday. This lovely summer evening.
These busy bodies building lives
in which to row themselves toward a horizon
that approaches regardless. This November
firepit in the backyard. This clear night filling
with our shouts and smoke swirls. The late sunrise
that signals winter. Headlines clicking away.

The delicately crazy wander their workplaces
with a smile on and always a task to carry out, their minds
full of knives and fears and a need to be needed. I wish
I was better at inciting in people a lightheartedness.
That I was better at laughter. At my job there is a middle-
aged woman who acts like a child. She must
have her reasons. She said, once, in casual
conversation, that she didn't want to die. She would
miss everyone. No, you won't, someone
corrected her.

What was left of the human world were mute
shapes. Text on screens. Battery lights
beeping in the shade of trees. Men fall
on their backs and stare at the sky for hours
for there's little else to do in a land that can't
remember itself. Let the underwater
cities we never saw stay as they are. Our radio-
active waste will outlive our methods
of containing it safely. We have centuries
to stumble through. The blood of our words
is still fresh on our clothes.

Little girl stands under street lamp and sings
to the planes in the sky.
Below the oval windows of those big machines
the world turns slow and massive.
All that blue distance traveled by the eye. Bluebird
on a branch watching me fumble my thoughts
as my washing machine clatters cheerfully in the night.
At the airport, a father waits at the bottom of the escalators
with his creased face and his lifetime's worth
of lessons, which he himself in his quiet way
is trying still to learn.

It was raining and the people at the station
were huddled under the customer service booth's
big awning. High school girls with backpacks
and stickered folders. Stout Mexican mothers. Children
staring at the shimmering ground. Old men lost in thoughts
of other lives. Sheets of rain drifting across everything.
This was February. Year of war and recession. Still
no other species to talk to. After some minutes,
a bus came and got everyone. Rain began
gathering in streams against the curbs.

I remember you crawling into bed like a child, eyes
half-closed, ready for sleep. After two years, the space
you take up inside me is finally growing small.
There are just too many people crowding in.
Your voice surfaces clear in my mind only, it seems,
when it's winter and I'm lonely and it's just me
and your memory in a small room. This December
I've thought about you every day like a cat
watching the rain fall. Have wondered if I live still,
somewhere in there, wherever you are.

Girl with leopard-print boots listens to headphones
while ignoring the catcalls of boys sitting nearby.
At night, in the park, a man offers blow to passing women
by way of courtship. Two teenagers lie on the roof
of a suburban house and watch the moon.
Coyotes make their sounds in the field below.
A two-lane road atop the low ridge dissecting the town
fills on one side with red brake lights. A step
holds our histories but, too, the possibility
of weightless action. On a morning walk, the dry grass
bending round the shape of the shoe's sole. Dragonflies
darting through the holes of a chain-link fence.

He only liked to play and sing outside.
The modern indoors, the neat, too brightly lit
apartments were not right for music.
The weather's embrace is a giver of moods.
In it he could throw his vocal cords' vibrations
into the air where the insects live and the tall
buildings in the distance interrupt the sky.
He sang of our lives colliding and parting,
the broken off pieces flying out over the trees
and the houses to land in strangers' yards
like flecks of skin.

We didn't even have to burn the bridges. We just
forgot what they were for. Some of the villagers
learned to manipulate numbers, beautiful, mercurial
numbers, and they never again set foot on earth.
Some of us landed in cities so devoid of empathy
that we stayed in our rooms sometimes for months
as if they were wombs that could safely strip
back our lives. We wanted to be nothing again,
and yet our lusts kept blooming forth their terrible
creations.

They were drunk, on the grass, their limbs
warm and loose, their act's consequences
so far ahead they could not feel them, like distant
fires whose potential to harm is lost on the child
observing from afar, entranced by the glow
of the flames.   Collided particles
have no chance of untangling their fates.
And yet we must live as if our movements
through space are undecided. Twisting in our
heads while the night passes. Waking up to fog
and walking into it.

ABOUT THE AUTHOR

Jesús Castillo was born in 1986 in San Luis Potosí, Mexico. He moved to California with his parents and sister in 1998. In 2009, he graduated from the University of California-San Diego where he studied literature and writing. Castillo helped organize 'Lectric Collective, an art and poetry collaboration in the Bay Area, and he was a founding editor of *Vertebrae*. He has lived in Oceanside, La Jolla, Oakland, San Francisco, and Iowa City where he received an MFA in poetry from the University of Iowa.

ACKNOWLEDGMENTS

Special thanks to the editors of *elimae*, *Sparkle&Blink*, *California Northern*, and *Out of Our*, where sections from this book have appeared. I want to thank my parents and sister for their constant support, as well as Jesse Nathan for his invaluable friendship and work as editor. Special thanks also to Evan Karp, for his support and for being one of the first to provide the poem with an audience; and to Jillian Roberts, the 'Lectric Collective, and Kyle Peeck: their feedback and encouragement, especially in the early stages of the manuscript, was more helpful than I can say. Finally, thank you Eden V. Evans—your faith in me when I needed it made finishing the book almost easy.

THE McSWEENEY'S POETRY SERIES

1. *Love, an Index* by Rebecca Lindenberg (2012).

2. *Fragile Acts* by Allan Peterson (2012).

3. *City of Rivers* by Zubair Ahmed (2012).

4. *x* by Dan Chelotti (2013).

5. *The Boss* by Victoria Chang (2013).

6. *TOMBO* by W. S. Di Piero (2014).

7. *Morning in Serra Mattu: A Nubian Ode* by Arif Gamal (2014).

8. *Saint Friend* by Carl Adamshick (2014).

9. *Tradition* by Daniel Khalastchi (2015).

10. *Remains* by Jesús Castillo (2016).

THE
McSWEENEY'S POETRY SERIES

The McSweeney's Poetry Series is founded on the idea that good poems can come in any style or form, by poets of any age anywhere. Our goal is to publish the best, most vital work we can find, regardless of pedigree. We're after poems that move, provoke, inspire, delight—poems that tear a hole in the sky. And when we find them, we'll publish them the only way we know how: in beautiful hardbacks, with original artwork on the cover. These are books to own, books to cherish, books to loan to friends only in rare circumstances.

≫—≪

SUBSCRIPTIONS

The McSweeney's Poetry Series subscription includes our next four books for only $40—an average of $10 per book—delivered to your door, shipping included. You can sign up at store.mcsweeneys.net

≫—≪

PREVIOUS TITLES

Tradition by Daniel Khalastchi
"Khalastchi's poetry radiates like a nuclear transmitter."
—Cathy Park Hong

Saint Friend by Carl Adamshick
"These are poems of great substance, powered by great love.
I applaud *Saint Friend*." —Albert Goldbarth

Morning in Serra Mattu: A Nubian Ode by Arif Gamal
"Each poem in *Morning in Serra Mattu* is an epistle
of longing and memory." —Yusef Komunyakaa

TOMBO by W. S. Di Piero
"A superb poet." —Gerald Stern